D0567959

T2-BPV-768

EYEWITNESS
CAT

Jaguar

Serval

Tabby cat

Plaque showing a crowned
lion, Limoges, 12th century

Tigers

19th-century inlaid
earthenware tile

EYEWITNESS
CAT

Written by
Juliet Clutton-Brock

Abyssinian
kittens

Ocelot

Abyssinian

Maine coon

Black
leopard

Ginger-and-white cat

Puma cub

Ginger cat

Black-and-white cat

Bobcat

Lion

LONDON, NEW YORK,
MELBOURNE, MUNICH, AND DELHI

Project editor Gillian Denton
Art editor Thomas Keenes
Senior editor Helen Parker
Senior art editor Julia Harris
Production Louise Barratt
Picture research Diana Morris
Special photography Dave King
Additional special photography Philip Dowell,
Colin Keates ABIPP

RELAUNCH EDITION (DK UK)
Editor Ashwin Khurana
US editor Margaret Parrish
Senior designers Rachael Grady, Spencer Holbrook
Managing editor Gareth Jones
Managing art editor Philip Letsu
Publisher Andrew Macintyre
Producer, preproduction Adam Stoneham
Senior producer Charlotte Cade
Jacket editor Maud Whatley
Jacket designer Laura Brim
Jacket design development manager Sophia MTT
Publishing director Jonathan Metcalf
Associate publishing director Liz Wheeler
Art director Phil Ormerod

RELAUNCH EDITION (DK INDIA)
Senior editor Neha Gupta
Art editors Deep Shikha Walia, Dhirendra Singh
Senior DTP designer Harish Aggarwal
DTP designers Anita Yadav, Pawan Kumar
Managing editor Alka Thakur Hazarika
Managing art editor Romi Chakraborty
CTS manager Balwant Singh
Jacket editorial manager Saloni Talwar
Jacket designers Govind Mittal, Suhita Dharamjit, Vikas Chauhan

First American Edition, 1991
This American Edition, 2014
Published in the United States by DK Publishing
4th floor, 345 Hudson Street
New York, New York 10014

14 15 16 17 18 10 9 8 7 6 5 4 3 2 1
196433—07/14

ISBN 978-1-4654-2050-3 (Paperback)
ISNB: 978-1-4654-2092-3 (ALB)

DK books are available at special discounts when purchased in bulk for sales promotions,
premiums, fund-raising, or educational use. For details, contact: DK Publishing Special
Markets, 345 Hudson Street, New York, New York 10014 or SpecialSale@dk.com.
Color reproduction by Alta Image Ltd., UK
Printed by South China Printing Co. Ltd., China

Discover more at

www.dk.com

Early Greek gold
necklace plate

Puma

Contents

Leopard

What is a cat?

Cats are possibly the most beautiful and graceful of all animals. They have fine fur, which is often strikingly marked with spots or stripes (p. 14), and elegant heads with pointed ears and large eyes. Wild and domestic cats all belong to one family, the Felidae. Cats have all the typical features of mammals: they are warm-blooded, have a protective skeleton, and produce milk to feed their young. All cats are carnivores, or meat-eaters, and they almost all live and hunt on their own. The exception is the lion (pp. 28–29), which hunts in a family group, or pride. Affectionate, intelligent, and playful, the domestic cat is one of the most popular of all animal companions.

Good and evil
In Christian communities, cats have always represented both good and evil. Here, good and bad cat spirits fight over the soul of a cat woman.

Now you see me...
This jaguar is well hidden. The striped and spotted fur of the cat family provides very effective camouflage in forests, jungles, grasslands, and plains.

Lindisfarne Gospels
The beautiful Lindisfarne Gospels were written and decorated in Britain in around 700 CE. Domestic cats were clearly familiar animals at this time.

Adaptation
Domestic cats are very adaptable. They are found all over the world, from tropical Africa to icy Greenland. The domestic cat is the only member of the cat family that lives and breeds happily within human society.

The stripes and markings of this domestic cat are inherited from its wild ancestor

Whiskers are organs of touch and help all cats—big, small, wild, or domestic—to feel objects in the dark

Cats in Japan
The Japanese have a definite sympathy with the mysterious cat. In art, they have often shown its changeable nature by portraying one cat made up of many others.

The mane of the adult male lion is the only obvious sign of sexual difference in the whole cat family

Cooperative cat
Lions live and hunt with other members of their pride. Like all cats, lions kill their prey by stalking their victim, then leaping on it and biting into its neck (pp. 28–29).

All cats have claws and all except the cheetah sheathe them when at rest (pp. 42–43)

Rudyard Kipling
This British writer described the cat's need for solitude in his story called *The Cat that Walked by Himself.*

The first cats

Millions of years ago, many catlike animals roamed the Earth, some more massive and fierce than any alive today. The earliest fossil ancestors of the cat family come from the Eocene period, some 50 million years ago. These evolved into the species of large and small cats that are living today. There were also the now-extinct, saber-toothed cats named after their enlarged, daggerlike canine teeth. The best-known is the American species *Smilodon*.

Stuck on you
In the Ice Age, an eruption of black, sticky tar at Rancho La Brea, now part of modern Los Angeles, trapped thousands of animals, including 2,000 saber-toothed *Smilodon*.

Tooth root extends some distance into the skull

Thylacosmilus
Thylacosmilus looked like a saber-toothed cat, but was not part of the cat family. It was a mammal that lived in South America during the Pliocene era about five million years ago.

Very large teeth used for biting off chunks of meat

Huge saber teeth used as daggers to stab prey

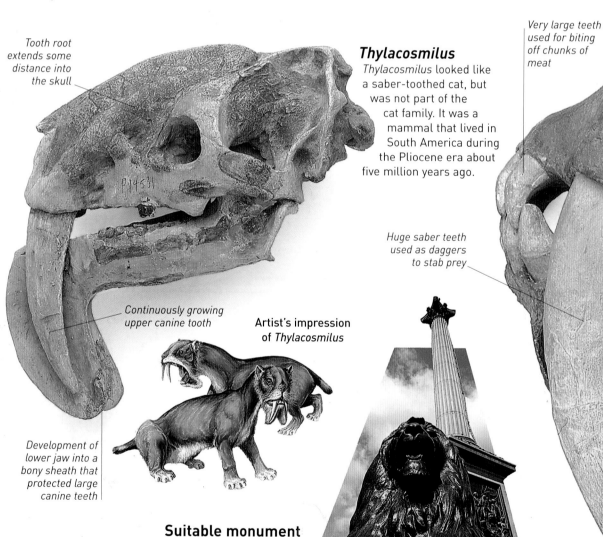

Continuously growing upper canine tooth

Artist's impression of *Thylacosmilus*

Development of lower jaw into a bony sheath that protected large canine teeth

Suitable monument
Sir Edwin Landseer (1802–1873) sculpted the lions in London's Trafalgar Square to commemorate British victories in battle. During the last Ice Age, real lions existed in Britain, and some of their bones have been found right underneath the Landseer sculptures.

Smilodon

This large, saber-toothed cat lived on open grasslands in family groups and preyed on large herd animals. *Smilodon* became extinct about 14,000 years ago.

econstruction
f *Smilodon.*
o one knows
s true color

Smilodon *was small-brained and most of its skull was made up of jaws and teeth*

Miacis

This animal was one of the most distant ancestors of the cat family. It probably lived in tropical forests about 50 million years ago. *Miacis* has been found as a fossil in Germany.

The stabber

Smilodon's saber teeth extended well below the lower jaw, so the animal could use them without opening its mouth wide. The teeth were used like daggers to stab prey. All the saber-tooths had slightly weaker lower jaws, but the muscles used to bring the head down could exert a powerful force that was essential for stabbing huge, slow-moving animals.

Weak lower jaw

Dinictis

A little like *Hoplophoneus* but smaller, *Dinictis* was probably a grassland predator. It has been found as a fossil in South Dakota.

Stabbing tooth

Hoplophoneus

This was one of the earliest extinct cats. It lived in North America 35 million years ago. This cat was only distantly related to *Smilodon*, but it had similar large, canine teeth for stabbing prey.

Cat clans

Cats kill other animals for food and so belong to the order Carnivora (flesh-eaters). There are four groups within the cat family: the small cats, which include domestic cats, the black-footed cat, and the puma; the large cats, (the lion, the tiger, the jaguar, the leopard, and the snow leopard); and two groups with only one cat each—the cheetah and the clouded leopard. Cats have highly developed senses, fast movements, and very sharp teeth. Unlike the large cats, the small cats are unable to roar. The domestic cat is descended from a species of small wild cat, *Felis silvestris*, which can still be found in Europe, western Asia, and Africa.

Origin of the species
Swedish botanist Carl von Linné (Linnaeus) invented the system of giving Latin names to plants and animals.

Puma
The puma, or cougar, is an oversized small cat that can purr like a tabby. It lives in North and South America.

Bobcat
The bobcat is the most common wild cat in North America. It looks a little like a lynx, without the long ear tufts.

Domestic cat
There are almost as many breeds of domestic cat as there are dog breeds.

Small cats

All the small cats (including the smaller wild cats) live on their own and hunt by night. They are found all over the world, and, tragically, many have been hunted almost to extinction for their beautifully patterned, soft furs.

Big cats

The big cats need a great deal of meat to survive. For this reason, they have always been fewer in number than the small cats, who are more able to find enough food for their needs.

On the air
One of the most famous advertising cats is the MGM lion, seen here practicing his roar.

Tiger
The tiger is the largest and heaviest of all the cats. It is a night hunter and preys on animals smaller than itself. Tigers are found from tropical India to icy Siberia.

Not like the others

The clouded leopard does not roar like the other big cats, nor does it groom or rest like a small cat. The cheetah is unique because it is a running cat (pp. 42–43), whereas all others are leaping cats.

Clouded leopard
The clouded leopard lives in the forests of Southeast Asia, but it is rarely seen and is in danger of extinction.

Cheetah
Cheetahs do not have sheaths over their claws and can run at great speed. This has helped them to adapt to life on the grasslands of Africa, where many animals compete for food.

Ancestors
of early cats

Social
hunters

Solitary
hunters

Leaping
cats

Running
cats

Lion   Other   Clouded   Small   Cheetah
        big cats leopard   cats

The descent of the cat
In this diagram, the cheetah is separated from all the other cats because it is the only one able to chase its prey at great speed. However, like other cats, it still kills its prey by leaping on it and biting its neck. All other cats are called leaping cats, because they slowly stalk their prey and then pounce.

The bare bones

A cat's skeleton consists of about 250 bones. It protects the soft parts of the body, while allowing the cat to move with great agility. The skull is specially designed for killing prey. The eye sockets are round to allow a wide field of vision, the hearing parts are large, and the short, strong jaws open very wide. Cats kill their prey with their very sharp canine teeth and then cut pieces off with their carnassial (shearing) teeth.

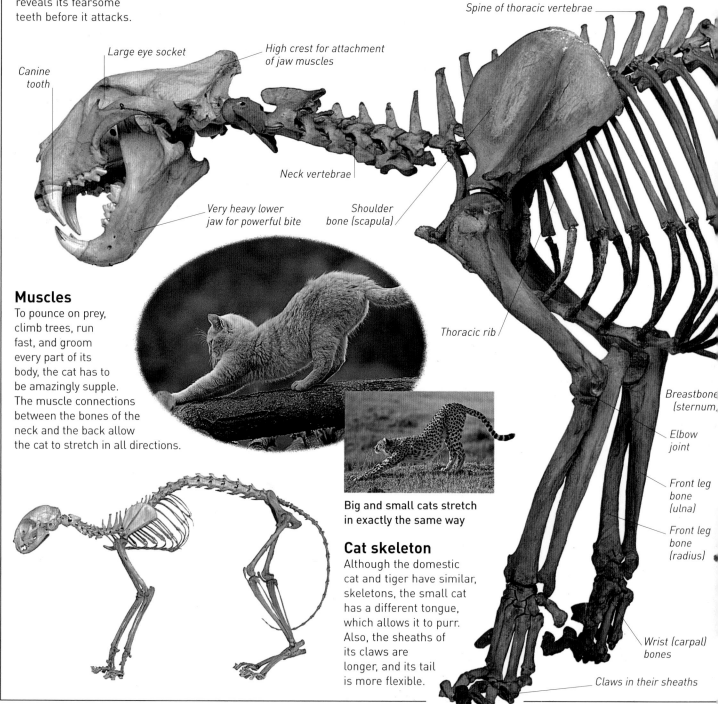

Night prowler
This snow leopard reveals its fearsome teeth before it attacks.

Canine tooth

Large eye socket

High crest for attachment of jaw muscles

Spine of thoracic vertebrae

Neck vertebrae

Very heavy lower jaw for powerful bite

Shoulder bone (scapula)

Thoracic rib

Muscles
To pounce on prey, climb trees, run fast, and groom every part of its body, the cat has to be amazingly supple. The muscle connections between the bones of the neck and the back allow the cat to stretch in all directions.

Big and small cats stretch in exactly the same way

Cat skeleton
Although the domestic cat and tiger have similar, skeletons, the small cat has a different tongue, which allows it to purr. Also, the sheaths of its claws are longer, and its tail is more flexible.

Breastbone (sternum)

Elbow joint

Front leg bone (ulna)

Front leg bone (radius)

Wrist (carpal) bones

Claws in their sheaths

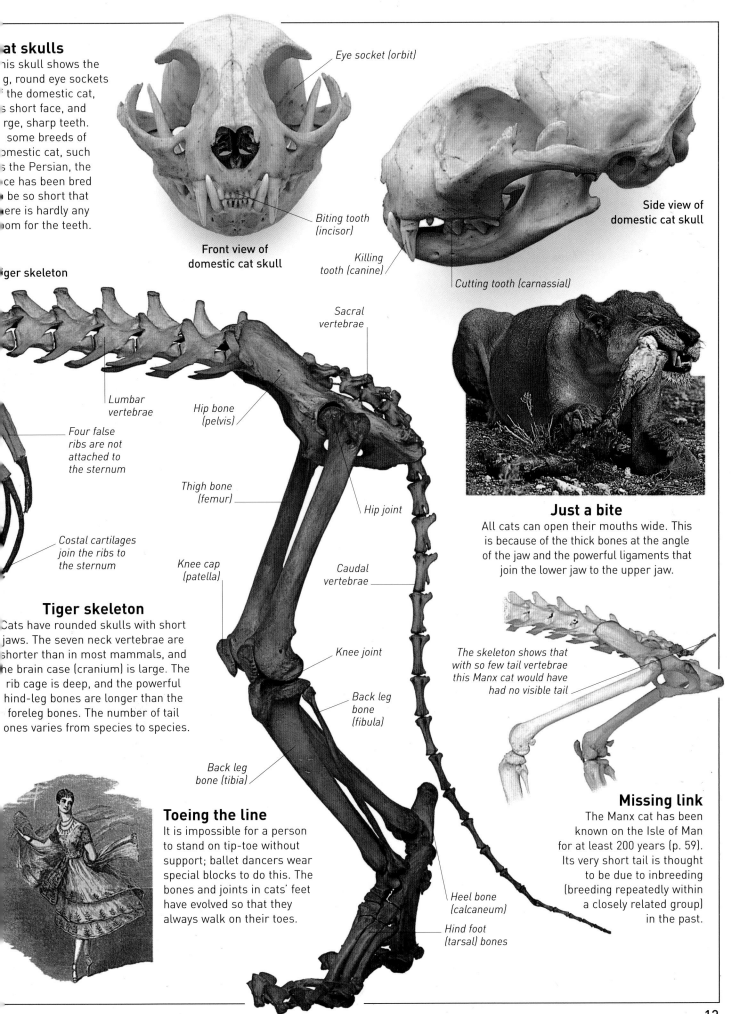

at skulls

his skull shows the
g, round eye sockets
the domestic cat,
short face, and
rge, sharp teeth.
some breeds of
omestic cat, such
the Persian, the
ce has been bred
be so short that
ere is hardly any
om for the teeth.

Eye socket (orbit)

Side view of
domestic cat skull

Biting tooth
(incisor)

Front view of
domestic cat skull

Killing
tooth (canine)

Cutting tooth (carnassial)

iger skeleton

Sacral
vertebrae

Lumbar
vertebrae

Hip bone
(pelvis)

Four false
ribs are not
attached to
the sternum

Thigh bone
(femur)

Hip joint

Just a bite

All cats can open their mouths wide. This
is because of the thick bones at the angle
of the jaw and the powerful ligaments that
join the lower jaw to the upper jaw.

Costal cartilages
join the ribs to
the sternum

Knee cap
(patella)

Caudal
vertebrae

Tiger skeleton

Cats have rounded skulls with short
jaws. The seven neck vertebrae are
shorter than in most mammals, and
he brain case (cranium) is large. The
rib cage is deep, and the powerful
hind-leg bones are longer than the
foreleg bones. The number of tail
ones varies from species to species.

Knee joint

Back leg
bone
(fibula)

The skeleton shows that
with so few tail vertebrae
this Manx cat would have
had no visible tail

Back leg
bone (tibia)

Toeing the line

It is impossible for a person
to stand on tip-toe without
support; ballet dancers wear
special blocks to do this. The
bones and joints in cats' feet
have evolved so that they
always walk on their toes.

Missing link

The Manx cat has been
known on the Isle of Man
for at least 200 years (p. 59).
Its very short tail is thought
to be due to inbreeding
(breeding repeatedly within
a closely related group)
in the past.

Heel bone
(calcaneum)

Hind foot
(tarsal) bones

Inside out

Cats have evolved so that they can feed on other live animals. They have to be fast thinkers, fast killers, and, in order to outwit other predators, fast eaters. Cats are very intelligent and their brains are large in relation to the size of their bodies. Their intestines are relatively short and simple because they need to digest only meat and not plant matter. After a kill, the wild cat will gorge itself on its prey, then it may go for several days before it needs to hunt again. The cat's rough tongue is used to scrape flesh from bones as well as to draw food into the mouth (p. 20).

Gene machine
The curly coat of this rex is an abnormality caused by inbreeding (p. 13). Inbreeding can lead to genetic changes in the offspring.

Flehmen
By curling back his upper lip in a special grimace (flehmen), the lion is using the Jacobson's (taste smell) organ (p. 16) to tell if there is a lioness ready to mate nearby.

Rounded head with short face

Lithe bo

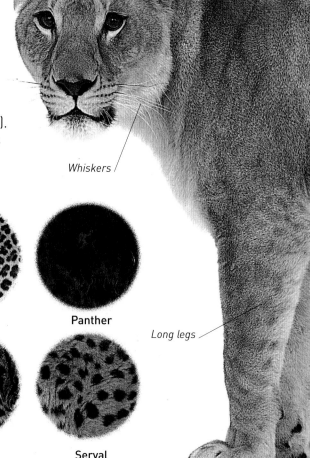

Fur

Fur keeps the cat warm, acts as camouflage, carries the animal's scent, and is sensitive to touch (pp. 16–17). All wild cats have an undercoat of fine, soft fur, covered by an outer coat of coarser, longer hairs (guard hairs). These outer hairs carry the coat's spotted or striped pattern.

Whiskers

Long legs

Spot me
The spotted coat of this leopard provides perfect camouflage in the sun-dappled, wooded grasslands. Only its tawny-yellow eyes can be seen, waiting for any movement that might mean food.

Tiger

Leopard

Panther

Jaguar

Ocelot

Serval

Fur coats
The furs on the right have very different patterns. For hundreds of years, people have used animal furs to make coats. Today, people realize that it is cruel to kill animals for their furs.

Claws

A cat's claws are made of keratin, a protein also found in human nails. The hind paws have four claws; the fore paws have five. The fifth claw helps the cat to grip when climbing or holding prey.

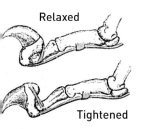

Relaxed

Tightened

Claws for concern

All cats except for cheetahs have sheathed claws. When the claws are relaxed, they are covered by a bony sheath (top). Special muscles extend the claws, and the toes spread out at the same time.

Bad kitty

This American illustration shows how a playful cat can inflict painful scratches.

Purr-fect communication

In the small cats, the set of bones at the base of the tongue is hard and bony, which allows them to purr. The sound is made when these bones vibrate. A cat usually purrs when it is relaxed and content.

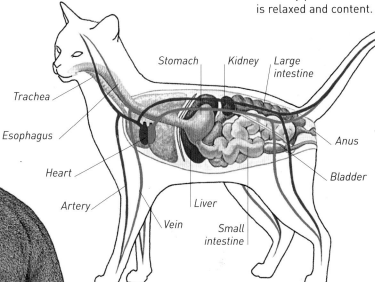

Stomach · Kidney · Large intestine

Trachea

Esophagus

Heart

Artery

Vein

Liver

Small intestine

Anus

Bladder

Cat's digestive system

A cat's food passes from the throat to the stomach via a passage called the esophagus. It then goes to the small intestine, where the nutrients are absorbed into the blood stream. Waste passes through the large intestine and out of the anus.

Long tail for balance

Good points

The muscular body of the lioness has a rounded head, a short face, and fairly long legs. The long tail helps the heavy cat to balance when she makes rapid changes of direction while chasing prey. Sensitive whiskers on the sides of her face help her to find her way around in the dark. The senses of sight, smell, hearing, and balance are particularly well developed in all cats, both big and small.

Muscles

The muscles in the cat's shoulders are very powerful and are used when the animal leaps onto its prey.

Supersenses

Most wild cats hunt at night. They have highly developed senses so that they can move quietly, see everything around them, hear the slightest noise, and smell any other animals in the dark. The small cat has to be alert, ready to flee if threatened. Cats have one sense that humans do not have, known as the "taste-smell" sense (p. 14). The homing instinct of cats is legendary and there are many stories of cats finding their way home over long distances.

Tight squeeze
Cats use their highly sensitive whiskers and guard (outer) hairs to judge distances. So if there is room for the fur, there is room for the cat's body.

Time for a drink
A puma drinks from a freshwater pool. All cats except the sand cat (p. 39) need water regularly.

The eyes have it
Cats have a layer of extra reflecting cells in their eyes called the *tapetum lucidum* (p. 64). These reflectors shine in the dark when a cat's eyes are caught in headlights.

Pupils expanded (above), narrowed (below)

Pupil power
A cat's eyes are round and can look in a wide angle all around the head. In darkness, the pupils expand widely to let in as much light as possible. In bright light, they narrow to tiny slits in small cats, or to tight circles in big cats.

Cell mates
In 1601, the Earl of Southampton was imprisoned in the Tower of London for rebelling against Elizabeth I. The story goes that his cat found its way alone across the city to the Tower. Once there, he crossed roofs until he found the room where the Earl was being held and climbed down the chimney. The story may well be true, because this portrait was painted at the time.

Stretch 'n' sniff
When cats are presented with food or any strange object, they are cautious. They may first reach out and tap it with a paw, before stretching out and exploring it with their noses.

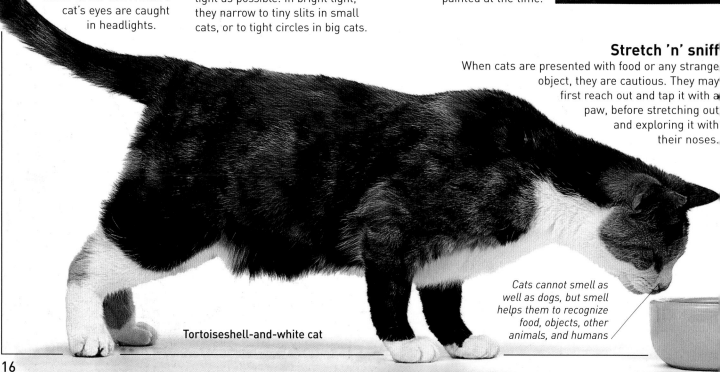

Tortoiseshell-and-white cat

Cats cannot smell as well as dogs, but smell helps them to recognize food, objects, other animals, and humans

Five senses

In all cats, the senses of sight, hearing, smell, taste, and touch are more highly developed than they are in humans. Although humans are more sensitive to color, cats can navigate better in the dark using their whiskers, feet, and very sensitive guard hairs.

Large, funnel-shaped ears draw sound waves into the inner ear, so that the cat can judge the direction of a noise

Eyes open wide when a cat is alert and interested and close to a slit when it is angry and frightened

Whiskers

Whiskers are long, stiff hairs with sensitive nerve endings at their roots. They spread out around the face of the cat so that it can feel where it is in relation to objects nearby. In bad light, they act as a backup to the cat's sight.

he nose, which has o fur covering, is a ery sensitive organ. draws in scents to receptors on many in, curled bones in e front of the skull

The rough tongue is used for grooming the coat, cleaning kittens, and lapping up liquids p. 20–21). A keen sense of taste is important, ecause as the cat bolts s meat, it must be able to distinguish quickly any part that might be rotten and harmful

Sorrel
Abyssinian

Magnificent movers

All cats are extremely agile and can leap with great power, although, except for the cheetah, they can run fast over only short distances (pp. 42–43). Unlike many other carnivores, the cat has collar bones, which prevent it from jarring its shoulders when it leaps from a height. The shoulder blades are placed at the sides of the cat's chest, which helps it to climb. Cats that spend a lot of time in trees, such as the leopard (pp. 32–33), have long tails for balance. All cats walk on their toes and their feet have thick, soft pads so they can move quietly.

Wild cat strike
A big cat is so powerful that it can kill with one lunge of a paw. This lion knows its strength and would never hurt another member of its pride.

Cat puts all four paws together for maximum power at takeoff

Cat is at full stretch in mid-leap

One giant leap...
Cats jump by flexing and relaxing the muscles of the limbs and back, while balancing with the tail. Unlike many other jumping animals, a cat can judge its landing position with great accuracy. This is essential for a hunter of fast-moving, small prey.

Cat balances on back paws as it begins leap

Puma cub

Nine lives
Cats can fall from great heights and always seem to land on their feet. Many of the small cats, as well as the leopard, spend much of their lives in trees. Their highly developed sense of balance helps them hunt fast-moving animals like squirrels, while creeping along a flimsy branch. The nervous system has evolved so that the cat can right itself midflight to keep from damaging its body on landing.

When running slowly, opposite legs go together—right foreleg and left hind leg move in unison

Practice
All cubs and kittens have to exercise their limbs and muscles before they can be as flexible as their parents. This young cub's paws seem too big for its body, but with practice it will soon be as agile as its mother.

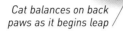

Running wild

When a cat runs, it pushes off with both back legs at the same time, but places the front paws down separately. Eadweard Muybridge took this famous sequence in 1887 to show how a cat moves when running.

Front paws land and cat begins to bring back paws forward

All four paws touch land

Cool cat

Few cats seem to enjoy swimming, except for tigers, who spend a fair amount of time in or near water. Tigers living in the tropical rain forests of Asia use the water to keep cool.

Tail is essential for balance like the pole carried by a tightrope walker

Up a gum tree

All kittens have to learn to climb. At first, they often venture too far up a tree and are then terrified of going up or down. After a few false starts, however, all but the most timid jump to the ground and land on their feet.

Loose skin, and muscles not yet developed

Balancing act

This cat shows how it can walk along the top of a very high, very narrow fence. It places its paws neatly one in front of the other and is never in danger of falling.

Cleaning up

Cats are exceptionally clean animals. They spend a lot of time licking their fur, pulling dirt from their feet, and wiping their faces with their paws. Grooming allows the cat to spread its scent all over its body and then to rub it onto people, objects, and other animals. It also helps the cat to relax. Domestic cats bury their droppings, unlike many wild cats, who deposit them in prominent positions to mark their territory (pp. 26–27). Licking, rubbing, and depositing droppings are all part of a cat's complex pattern of communication through smell and touch.

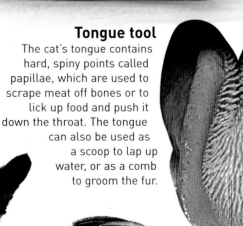

Most cats do not like water, but these kittens by cat artist Louis Wain (1860–1939) seem to be having fun

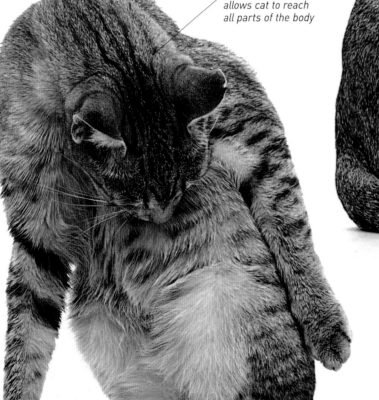

Flexibility of neck allows cat to reach all parts of the body

Tongue tool
The cat's tongue contains hard, spiny points called papillae, which are used to scrape meat off bones or to lick up food and push it down the throat. The tongue can also be used as a scoop to lap up water, or as a comb to groom the fur.

Belly brush-up
The cat licks its body to groom its fur and to strengthen its own scent after it has been stroked or has fed its kittens.

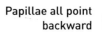

Papillae all point backward

Papillae, each shaped like a miniature tongue

Sponging down
This cat, by Japanese artist Ando Hiroshige (1797–1858), is washing its ears. This is sometimes said to be a sign that rain is on the way.

Paw thoroughly dampened for washing face

Washcloth
The cat licks its paw, then rubs its foot around its jaws. This spreads its scent from glands in the chin to its feet, so its scent will be left wherever it walks.

Paws for action
If a cat walks on something sticky, it will wash it off at once. Clean paws are essential for fast movement and climbing—but washing the paws also helps to spread the cat's scent.

The rough tongue wets the paw in order to wash the face

Reaching the parts...
These lionesses keep each other clean by licking parts they cannot easily reach themselves. More importantly, by spreading their personal scents over each other, they become familiar with other members of the pride. When cats want to show they belong together, they make sure they smell the same.

Personal hygiene
By grooming the inside of its leg, the cat is spreading scent from its chin and genital glands around its body.

Paws spread to give tongue maximum access

Hunting

In the wild, all cats feed on the animals they have killed. Cats are solitary hunters, except for the lion, which hunts in a group (pp. 28–29). Cats usually kill animals smaller than themselves, although sometimes they will attack a larger animal. Motionless animals sometimes escape attack, but with practice, cats can recognize prey by sound and scent alone. Cats stalk their prey, then leap on it and bite into its neck. Small cats feed mostly on mice, birds, and other small animals. Large cats, like the leopard, feed on bigger animals about the size of a goat. They often drag their prey up into trees to keep it away from other predators.

Tom and Jerry
In the famous cartoon, the cunning mouse Jerry often outwits the cat Tom—not often the case in real life.

A stalking cat holds its body close to the ground

Ready for action
This black leopard (also known as a panther) is stalking and getting ready for the kill. Every part of its body is on alert. All cats on the prowl move very slowly and silently until they are near enough to make a quick and decisive pounce.

The pads on a cat's paws help it to move silently

Medieval mousers
This medieval picture comes from a 13th-century book called *The Harleian Bestiary*. It is interesting because it is a very early illustration of cats with a rat.

In for the kill
Cats often choose a spot where they can see their prey without being seen. This cat would have been sitting absolutely still on the fence for some time, before leaping down on the unsuspecting prey.

Black panther

A fishy business
The fishing cat of India can flip fish out of the water with its slightly webbed paws and has even been seen diving for fish.

Telling tails
A cat lashes its tail when angry and twitches it gently to and fro when concentrating or contented.

Running down
The cheetah will not begin to hunt unless there is an antelope on its own. The antelopes know this and will not be disturbed unless the cheetah comes too close. Once the prey has been singled out, however, the cheetah will chase it at great speed.

A practiced killer
Many cats play with their prey before killing it. Mother cats often show their kittens how to hunt by capturing prey and then releasing it. Some cats keep this kittenish behavior in adult life.

A cat playing with a toy is reacting as if it were prey

Serval

Big meal
With its massive teeth, this tiger can snap a bone with one bite.

Chicken dinner
Small cats, like this serval, crouch down to eat their food. They begin by eating the head, which is swallowed whole with very little chewing. Big cats tend to eat lying down.

The young ones

Leopard with cubs in their den

The young of the large cats are usually called cubs, while the young of the small cats are called kittens. All cats are blind until they are at least nine days old. Domestic cats will choose a safe, dark spot like a drawer or closet to give birth, and there are usually about four kittens in a litter. Kittens take around 63 days to develop in the mother's womb (gestate), and after birth the mother gives them milk for six to eight weeks before they are weaned and begin to eat meat. In the wild, most cats give birth in a den. Lion cubs take between 100 and 119 days to gestate, and they are not weaned until they are three months old.

Knitting kitten
The kitten in this Japanese scroll is playing with a ball of yarn. Playing with toys helps kittens learn how to catch and hunt.

Lion king
When a lioness is in heat (ready to mate), the chief lion in a pride stays close to her, keeping other lions away. They mate many times over the next few days.

Family gathering
Although domestic cats may live in an apartment and have no contact with life in the wild, they still have all the instincts of wild cats. These kittens are now weaned, but the mother continues to protect and groom them. She also teaches them how to clean themselves and where to bury their waste.

Kitten grows adult coat of fine hairs over its wooly undercoat

Mating rituals
A female cat only allows a male to mate with her when she is in heat. In domestic cats, this usually happens twice a year. While in heat, the female may mate several times with different males (p. 61).

Identity crisis

Cubs and kittens often have differently marked coats from the adults. This spotted baby is, in fact, a puma. Its spots and stripes slowly fade as it grows up. Siamese kittens are born pale all over. The dark points only develop as the cat becomes an adult.

orrel
byssinian cat
nd kittens

Mother's rough tongue grooms kitten, helping it to understand about other cats' scents

Legs are slightly bandy and uncertain at first

Playing around

Play is an essential part of growing up. These kittens have to learn how to fight, but they must learn when to stop as well, so they are not hurt. Play also exercises the muscles of young animals and helps the brain to develop quick reactions.

Cub carriage

All mother cats are expert at carrying their young at the first hint of danger. This lioness grasps the loose skin around the neck of her cub between her teeth and carries the cub without hurting it at all.

Several pairs of teats for suckling— each kitten has its own teat and uses no other

Cat characteristics

All cats, whether wild or domesticated, behave in very similar ways. They give birth in safe, dark places, they exchange scents, and they hunt alone (except for the lion). They also all mark their territory by spraying urine and by depositing their droppings. Both large and small cats have various noises in common, such as meowing a greeting and yowling. All cats sleep a great deal, mostly in the day, so that they are ready for hunting at night. Unlike dogs, cats can rarely be trained; domestic cats have adjusted to living with humans, but they have never changed their essential character.

Lion lingo
The roar of the lion is one of the most frightening of all animal sounds. However, the lion roars as a means of communicating with the rest of the pride, rather than to frighten its prey.

Cat nap
Cats sleep a great deal. In hot countries, they may sleep up to 18 hours a day, hunting and feeding in the cooler hours. Cats usually sleep in several shortish periods, often with one eye partly open.

Friend...
Cats value their personal space. This cat feels that the other cat has come too close so she has crouched down in a defensive position.

Flattened ears are a warning sign

Hissing indicates tha this cat does not want to be bothered

Putting our heads together
Cats that live together, like domestic cats or lions, sometimes rub each other's heads to show that they have no intention of fighting.

Leggings
Cats often rub against people's legs to show affection and to transfer their scent.

Leaving a message

All cats mark their territory with urine and fluid from their glands. This is called spraying and they all do it in the same way. The cat backs up to a post or tree, lifts its rump high, and, with the tail held straight up, discharges a stream of strong-smelling fluid against the object.

Smartening up

Cats spend a good deal of their time "sharpening their claws." This is really stretching their limbs by digging their claws into a wooden tree (or silk-covered sofa!) and pulling the claws downward. The claws are probably not sharpened by this act, but they are cleaned, and the muscles of the feet and limbs are exercised.

Back slightly arched to make cat look bigger

Lioness scratching

Lions can tear the bark off a tree when "sharpening their claws."

Cat club

This fanciful illustration shows cats socializing. In real life, domestic cat colonies are based on the availability of food. They consist of related females, with a few dominant males.

Twitching tail shows that the cat is in an excited state

... Or foe?

Cats test each other's reactions with an explorative paw. Because this cat is getting a negative reaction from the tortoiseshell cat, he will probably back off.

Roly poly

All cats roll over on their backs to show affection or to show that a female is in heat (p. 24). They expose their bellies in this way only when they feel secure.

27

Top cat

Iranian plate
This plate shows a lion with the Sun rising behind it. This was the symbol of Iranian kingship.

More than 10,000 years ago, lions roamed the whole of Europe, Asia, and Africa. Aside from a small number in northwest India, lions today are found only in Africa. They live in family groups, or prides, of up to 12 animals. Because they hunt together, they are the only cats able to kill animals larger than themselves. Male lions defend their territory by pacing around it, roaring, and spraying their urine. The females are the main hunters. Each lioness will give birth to about five cubs every two years. If a new lion takes over a pride, he may kill any cubs a lioness has before he mates with her.

The king
His magnificent mane, heavy body, and huge canine teeth ensure that the lion rules his world. Males are always allowed to feed first at a kill.

African lion and lioness

Having no mane helps the lioness to hunt

The pride
Females always outnumber males in a pride. When a young male reaches adulthood, the resident male usually drives him away. He will then join a group of females in need of a male. The male's main role is to defend the pride's territory.

Mate to king
The lionesses are the core of any pride, and they stick close to their female relatives. They have strong, lithe bodies and creep stealthily before moving in for the kill.

Star sign of Leo
People born under Leo are said to be proud, brave, and strong, just like the lion itself.

The lions' den

In the Old Testament, Daniel was taken to the court of King Nebuchadnezzar as a captive. He was cast into the lions' den, but because God was on his side, the lions did not harm him.

The mane makes the lion look bigger than he really is. It may help to frighten off other lions

The lion and the unicorn

In the 15th and 16th centuries, lions often appeared in paintings. In this tapestry, the lion is shown to be at peace with the unicorn.

Herakles

In Greek myth, Herakles had to perform 12 tasks. The first was to kill the Nemean lion, whose skin could not be pierced—so he choked it to death.

The tuft of hair at the knees makes the lion look even stronger

The still visible spots are a leftover from when the lioness was a cub

The tuft at the end of the tail is an important signal in communication

The tiger

Tigers are the biggest and most powerful cats. They used to live in the forests of India, Southeast Asia, and China. Today, these endangered creatures live in a few tropical forest reserves and in swamps, like the Ganges Delta in India. The largest tigers come from the icy forests of Siberia, but only between four and five hundred still live there. Their habitat has been slowly destroyed, and they have been poached for their skins and bone. Tigers hunt and defend their territories on their own. They spend a good deal of time keeping cool in or near rivers, and they often hide the carcasses of their prey in dense thickets or in water.

Storm tiger
In this painting by French artist Henri Rousseau (1844–1910), the tiger is well camouflaged.

Heavy beast
The lion may be called the king of the beasts because of its great mane and proud carriage, but the tiger is more awesome. Tigers in India weigh up to 575 lb (260 kg) and the Siberian tiger is even heavier. Yet, despite their size, tigers live and hunt in the same way as all other cats.

The tiger's stripes camouflage it in long grass and forests

Very long, closely striped tail

Heavy b[...] is close [...] the grou[...] so the tiger car[...] be hidde[...] in grass[...] or water

Mass murder
In India, the tiger was always respected until the mid-19th century, when the British took power. During this time, huge numbers of tigers were slaughtered at shooting parties. Today, the tiger is again respected, and the Indian government has set up *Project Tiger* to save it from extinction.

Taking a ride

A mosaic tile, dating from the first to second century CE, was discovered in London, England. It shows Bacchus, the Roman god of wine, calmly riding a tiger.

Tiger by a torrent

This scroll, painted by Japanese artist Kishi Ganku (1756–1838), shows a fierce tiger beside a raging torrent.

The stripes on the back are more dispersed

Rounded head with long whiskers

Man-eating tigers

Tigers do not usually kill humans, although it can happen. It may be because the animal is injured and can no longer kill wild animals. Or it may be that people working in their territories have scared off the tigers' natural prey. In India, the government is doing all it can to keep people and tigers apart.

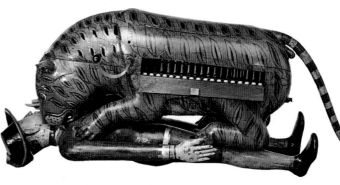

Tippu's tiger

This large mechanical "toy" was made during the Mogul Empire (1526–1857) in India. When the handle is turned, the tiger attacks the English soldier.

The huge paw is so powerful, that it can knock prey over with one blow

Face to face

Tigers usually attack from behind, so Indian farmworkers wear face masks on the back of their heads to confuse the cats.

Tree climber

Leopards live in the wooded grasslands of Africa and southern Asia. Although bulky, they are skilled climbers and can scale vertical trunks with complete ease. Leopards are secretive animals and stealthy hunters. They may occasionally prey on domestic farm animals, but they also kill animals, such as baboons and cane rats that destroy crops. Cubs are looked after by the mother until they are about two years old. Leopards are under threat everywhere, mainly because of the destruction of their habitat, but also because they have very desirable fur.

Treetop pantry
Leopards often carry their prey into trees. This protects the carcasses from hyenas and jackals, who would soon scrounge the food from the solitary leopard if it were left on the ground.

Leopards do not often roar but communicate by means of a rasping bark

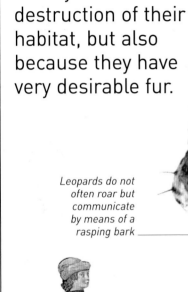

The Journey of the Magi
This painting by Gozzoli was commissioned by Piero de Medici for the chapel of his family palace in Florence, Italy. The Medicis kept leopards for hunting.

Leopard
The black spots on a tawny-yellow background act as a perfect camouflage for this shy animal as it hides in the dappled leaves of a tree or in the long, dry grass. As with most animals, the coat is short and sleek in countries where the climate is hot, but becomes much thicker and warmer in colder climates.

Spotless

The black panther is just a leopard with hidden spots. Its color comes from the combination of its genes. The panther behaves just like spotted leopards and breeds freely with them.

Panther
You can just see the spots on this panther's coat. This type of coat is most common in Southeast Asia.

Bagheera
Bagheera, the black panther, played an important part in Rudyard Kipling's *The Jungle Book*.

Snow leopard
This very rare, large cat is not the same species as the true leopard. A solitary hunter, it lives only in the high mountains of central Asia.

The spots look much better on a leopard than on a fur coat

The leopard's tail is long and darkly ringed

The soft-looking paw hides sharp claws used for killing prey and climbing trees

Benin bronze
This bronze plaque was made in the Bini kingdom in Nigeria in the 16th or 17th century. Known as the King of the Bush, the leopard was an important animal in Benin folklore. It was chosen as the king of the animals for its power, beauty, good nature, and wisdom.

Water cat

The jaguar is the only large cat to be found in the Americas. It lives mainly in the tropical forests of South America, and until quite recently it was also fairly common in the Southern United States. Although it is now protected, the jaguar is in real danger of extinction because of the destruction of its forest habitat and overhunting. The jaguar is larger than a leopard, but not as agile. A solitary hunter, it kills tapirs, turtles, and other small animals. It can climb trees, but prefers to hunt on the ground or in water.

Jaguar
This engraving shows the sturdy body of the jaguar.

Peruvian pot
Jaguars often featured in South American myths. This pot from Peru shows a jaguar eating its victim.

Ringed spots merge to blotches on the belly

Long tail helps the jaguar to balance

Grunter hunter
The jaguar is not as bold as the leopard, and it is generally slower. Unlike most big cats, it rarely roars. It grunts frequently when hunting and growls when threatened. Jaguars have sometimes been tamed, and occasionally they have even been known to live in a house!

Aquacat

Jaguars swim well and have been known to kill crocodiles. The Amazon peoples believe that jaguars lure fish to the surface by twitching their tails in the water. They then flip the fish out with their paws. River turtles are also a favorite food.

Knight cats

Mexican Aztec warriors belonged to either the order of the eagles or the jaguars. Each year warriors paraded in a military display. Jaguar knights wore a jaguar skin with the head used as a helmet.

Tapir trapper

Tapirs were once an important part of the jaguar's diet. They live in the Amazon forests, but tapirs are very scarce today.

Spotted head held low

Reddish-colored spots. Forest jaguars are darker than those living in grasslands

Short, massively powerful foreleg

The heavy body of the jaguar is a bit like a lion's

Tiahuanaco tapestry

This Peruvian tapestry, made approximately 1,000 years ago, illustrates the importance of the jaguar in Peruvian society. It shows a full-face jaguar head, flanked by two standing jaguars.

High society

Elizabethan lynx
This lynx was illustrated 500 years ago in England.

The lynx, bobcat, and puma, or cougar, are called small cats, although they are not particularly small—the puma, in fact, is the largest of all the small cats. The lynx and the bobcat are different from other cats in that they both have very short tails. The bobcat lives in North America, the lynx in Europe, North America, and Asia, and the puma in North and South America. All three are most at home high up on rocky mountain slopes.

Trapped
Hunting for bobcat and lynx is still allowed in North America, and thousands of bobcats are caught for their fur every year, often in vicious traps like this.

Bobcat cleaning itself, by US artist John James Audubon (1785–1851)

Short, stumpy tail

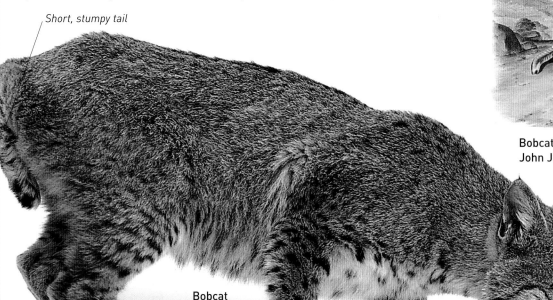

Bobcat

Unlike the lynx, the bobcat has only short tufts on its ears

Thick side-whiskers look a little like a mane

Bobcat
The bobcat's spotted coat camouflages it against rocks and bushy vegetation. Bobcats prey on small animals the size of hares. When mating, they caterwaul (howl) like domestic cats, but they are louder and more shrill. The female gives birth in a den lined with grass or moss and hidden in rocks.

The puma has a long, furry tail with a black tip, unlike the bobcat and the lynx

The hind legs are longer than the forelegs, making the puma a good stalker

The puma's coat can vary in color, but the underside is always pale

Lynx

The lynx is best adapted to life in high pine forests and thick scrub, where its brownish coat is invisible against moss and rocks. The long tufts on its ears are thought to help the lynx to hear well in dense forests. In winter, its big feet are covered with thick fur that acts like a snow shoe.

Lynx in summer coat

Lynx in winter coat

Sacred cat
In the Mochica culture of Peru around 600 BCE, the puma was worshiped as a god.

Puma

The puma is as much at home on the windswept shores of South America as on the Colorado mountains in the western US. It hides in rocky places and is a good climber. Pumas have large territories and cover long distances in search for prey.

Change of scenery
Although often found on mountains, pumas can also live in tropical rain forests.

The pupils are circular and do not contract to slits, as in the smaller cats

Puma

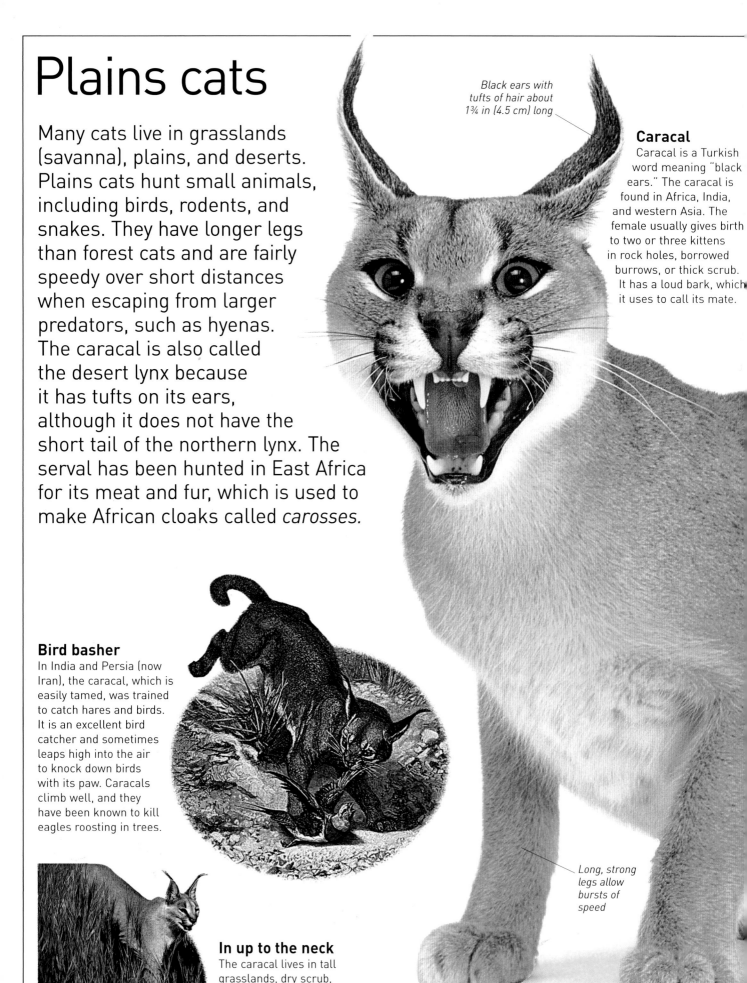

Plains cats

Many cats live in grasslands (savanna), plains, and deserts. Plains cats hunt small animals, including birds, rodents, and snakes. They have longer legs than forest cats and are fairly speedy over short distances when escaping from larger predators, such as hyenas. The caracal is also called the desert lynx because it has tufts on its ears, although it does not have the short tail of the northern lynx. The serval has been hunted in East Africa for its meat and fur, which is used to make African cloaks called *carosses*.

Black ears with tufts of hair about 1¾ in (4.5 cm) long

Caracal

Caracal is a Turkish word meaning "black ears." The caracal is found in Africa, India, and western Asia. The female usually gives birth to two or three kittens in rock holes, borrowed burrows, or thick scrub. It has a loud bark, which it uses to call its mate.

Bird basher

In India and Persia (now Iran), the caracal, which is easily tamed, was trained to catch hares and birds. It is an excellent bird catcher and sometimes leaps high into the air to knock down birds with its paw. Caracals climb well, and they have been known to kill eagles roosting in trees.

Long, strong legs allow bursts of speed

In up to the neck

The caracal lives in tall grasslands, dry scrub, and semidesert.

Serval
With its small head, spotted coat, and long legs, the African serval looks a little like a small cheetah. A good climber, it hunts small animals and catches birds. Servals always prefer to live near water.

Sand cat
The rarely seen sand cat lives in the Sahara and the deserts of western Asia. During the heat of the day, it sleeps in a dune burrow or under scrub. At night, it comes out to hunt lizards and mice. It can survive without water, getting sufficient liquid from its prey. The sand cat has thick, furry pads on its feet, so it can move fast over soft sand, and its yellow-brown coat blends into the desert.

Short, ringed tail with dark tip

Very long front legs good for speed

Short, dense fur keeps the cat warm at night and cool in the day

Tail is one-third of the length of the head and body

Black-footed cat
This fierce cat is the smallest of all wild cats. Named after the black soles of its feet, it lives in open, semidesert country in southern Africa.

Ocelot

Forest felines

Most of the small cats live in woodlands, forests, or jungles and are found on every continent except Australasia. Forest cats will eat pretty much anything that they are able to catch. They are almost all very striking in appearance, with powerful, agile bodies, spotted or striped fur, and huge eyes for night hunting (pp. 16–17). They are generally silent creatures but the males try to see off their enemies by caterwauling. All the species are in danger of extinction, both from loss of habitat and also because they are still hunted for their fur, particularly in South America.

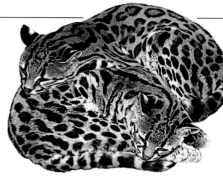

Margays
The margay looks like a smaller version of the ocelot, but it is slimmer, with longer legs and tail. It feeds on birds and lives in forest trees in South America.

Leopard cat
The leopard cat is the most common wild cat in southern Asia. It looks a lot like a domestic cat and is a good climber and swimmer. In China, they are known as money cats because their spots look like small coins.

Not a lotta ocelot!
Although mainly a forest cat, the ocelot is also found in grass and scrubland from Arizona to Argentina. Ocelots often live in pairs, hunt by day, and swim well. In Mexico, the ocelot is known as the "little tiger," thanks to its striped neck. It is the most hunted small cat in South America.

Ocelot

Flat-headed cat
This is a rare and elusive cat from India and Southeast Asia. It has dark brown fur tipped with white that gives it a silvery appearance. It appears to live along riverbanks, probably catching fish, frogs, birds, and small mammals.

Spots at the base of the tail become rings at the tip

Geoffroy's cat

Geoffroy's cat (named after its French discoverer, Étienne Geoffroy St. Hilaire) lives in forests and jungles in South America. It can live at high altitudes and is known as "the mountain cat" in Argentina. It often sleeps in trees during the day.

The dark spots are similar but smaller than those of the ocelot

Geoffroy's cat

The white ear spots are used to signal to other cats

The claws, hidden by the soft pads, are sharpened by climbing

Cutting back
If the destruction of the forests and jungles continues at the present rate, the balance of nature will be overturned forever and the beautiful cats that live in the forests will become extinct.

Speed king

The cheetah is the fastest land animal in the world. Unlike other cats, which are all leaping cats (pp. 10–11), the cheetah is called a running cat because it hunts fast-running animals. For this reason it is in a different group from all other cats and has a different Latin name, *Acinonyx jubatus*. The cheetah stalks its prey in the usual way, but then, at very high speed, it will chase after the gazelle or antelope and kill it with a sharp bite to the neck. It also preys on hares, guinea fowl, and even ostriches. The female cheetah lives alone, allowing males near only when she is in heat (p. 24). Male cheetahs often live in small groups, but only the dominant male will mate with a female.

Small head with short, rounded ear

Fast forward
The cheetah's long legs and flexible backbone enable it to run at speeds of up to 60 mph (100 kph). From a standing start, it can reach its top speed in three seconds.

No contest
The acceleration of a cheetah is comparable to this powerful Ferrari, although the animal can only keep up its speed for about 550 ft (170 m).

No cover-up
The cheetah needs to have extended claws when running to help it grip the ground. So, unlike other cats, the cheetah does not have a protective sheath over each claw.

Slender, long legs

Narrow, doglike paws

Wandering ways

The female hides her cubs in long grass while they are very young. She does not have a permanent den, so moves the cubs around every few days.

Supple, muscular back

Powerful hindquarters

Indian takeout

In the past, cheetahs were often trained to help hunters kill antelope and gazelle. Indian paintings of the 16th century show the cheetahs' role. They were sent to knock down prey, then they would wait for their owners to complete the kill.

Rare animals

Cheetahs are becoming very rare. In wildlife parks they are disturbed by tourists, and they are still being killed by poachers for their fur. Cheetahs used to be found across Africa and into India, but today they live mainly in Namibia and Zimbabwe. Cheetahs hunt by day and usually drag the carcasses into bushes to hide them from other animals.

The striped tail is more than half the length of the head and body

All furred up

Cheetahs have thicker fur on the neck and shoulders. It forms a sort of "mane" that can be seen in cubs, but not in adults.

Merger

The king cheetah of southern Africa is a very rare variety. The spots on its coat join to form stripes on its back.

Cats' kin

The many different breeds of domestic cat are descended from one wild species called *Felis silvestris*, the wildcat. This small cat can be found in European forests, African savanna, and the rocky lands of western Asia and India. In northern Europe, the wildcat has a stocky body and thick fur to cope with the cold climates. In Africa, the cat has a finer body, longer legs, and short hair. In India, the Indian desert cat lives in hot, dry country, and it is usually spotted. The wildcat shows many slight color variations, and the female is usually paler than the male. The African wildcat is most likely the ancestor of the domestic cat.

Broader head and longer face than a domestic cat's

Shortish tail with blunt end

Scottish wildcat

Wild in the highlands
This wildcat can be found in small numbers in Scottish forests, but it is in danger of extinction because it interbreeds with domestic cats that are living wild (pp. 60–61).

Wee wildcats
Kittens go hunting with their mother at about 12 weeks and are independent at about five months. Scottish wildcat kittens are very difficult to tame.

Out of Africa
African wildcats live in a range of habitats across Africa. They are not as shy as other wildcats and often live close to villages, interbreeding with domestic cats.

Not choosy
The Indian desert cat interbreeds with the northern wildcat, the African wildcat, and the domestic cat. It has a long, black-tipped tail and the soles of its feet are black. It lives in hot, dry places and hunts mice and lizards.

omestic cat
he domestic tabby is not ery different from its wild ncestor in its looks nd behavior.

Close relatives
The civet and the genet are not true cats, although they behave like them They are carnivores and belong to the mongoose family. Their heads look similar to those of cats, but their skulls are different.

Genet
Although its head is similar to a cat's, the genet's tail is very different.

Civet
The civet and the genet live in forests and hunt at night. They have spotted or striped bodies.

Ragged ears probably indicate many battles

Indian desert cat

The taming of the cat

Cats probably began living near human settlements to catch the rats and mice that were feeding on stored grain. People soon saw that cats were useful and encouraged them to remain. No one knows when cats first started living with humans, but it was probably at least 5,000 years ago. At the height of the Egyptian civilization 3,000 years ago, the cat was already a common domestic animal and eventually it became one of the most sacred animals in Egypt. It is, therefore, possible that the cat was first domesticated in ancient Egypt. Today, there are domestic cats in every part of the world where there are humans.

Mummified pet
When one of the sacred cats of ancient Egypt died, its body was mummified (treated to prevent decay), wrapped in bandages, and placed in a special tomb.

Persian puss
The fluffy, longhaired cat from Persia (now Iran) belongs to one of the oldest breeds of domestic cat, although this pot from the 13th century looks like a spotted cat rather the longhaired breed (pp. 56–57). Most longhaired pedigree cats today are descended from cats brought from Turkey and Iran in the 18th and 19th centuries.

Egyptian mau

Perfectly preserved
This mosaic of a cat with a bird was buried by volcanic ash when Mount Vesuvius erupted in Italy in 79 CE. It was found in almost perfect condition.

Ancient image
The spotted Egyptian mau is a domestic cat from Egypt. "Mau" is the ancient Egyptian word for cat. This is a new breed that first came to Europe in the 1950s, although with its graceful, body, green eyes, and pale coat, it looks very similar to the cats of ancient Egypt.

Fighting like cat and dog
These Greek men seem to be encouraging their animals to fight. The way the dog is standing, with its front legs squatting and its nose pushed forward, shows that it doesn't really want to fight, while the cat is arching its back ready to attack.

Catcher cat
This detail from an Egyptian tomb painting (from around 1400 BCE) shows a cat holding two birds in its claws and one in its mouth. It is helping its owner by retrieving the birds.

Cat goddess
The ancient Egyptians worshipped the goddess Bastet, who was usually shown as a woman with a cat's head. She often carried a *sistrum* (a musical instrument) and an *aegis* (a shield) decorated with a lioness's head.

As cats were seen as sacred in Egypt, they often appeared on jewelry, such as this gold ring

Slaying the serpent
Here, the Egyptian Sun god Ra, in the form of a cat, slays Apep, the serpent of darkness.

Myths and legends

Cats have always played a major role in folklore. This may be because they are such mysterious creatures: in the daytime they are often sleepy and affectionate, but at night they turn into stealthy, silent hunters. Many cats were killed in Europe in the late Middle Ages because they were thought to be linked with witchcraft.

Cats often play a prominent part in Russian fairy tales

But in eastern countries, such as Myanmar, their magical powers were praised. Cats were welcomed at sea, too, because many sailors believed that they could forecast storms.

Haunting tale
In Japan, cats have the power to turn into spirits when they die. This may be because in the Buddhist religion, the body of the cat is the temporary resting place of the soul of very spiritual people.

Blessed Birman
The Birman is the sacred cat of Myanmar. According to legend, the transformation of a white temple cat into a Birman helped to save a sacred temple from attack.

Cat chariot

During the early Renaissance period in Europe, cats were widely persecuted by the Christian Church. This was perhaps because of interest in the pagan Norse love goddess Freya, whose chariot was drawn by cats.

Familiar cats

In medieval times, the cat was thought to be a witch's "familiar" (her private connection with the devil). Many people also thought that witches could turn themselves into cats. Thousands of cats were burned in parts of Europe during this period.

Bond cat

Ernst Blofeld, the archenemy of spy James Bond, always had a white Persian cat at his side.

British black shorthair

Puss-in-Boots

In southern France, there was once a belief in *matagots* or magician cats. One of the most famous was Puss-in-Boots, created by Charles Perrault.

Black magic

Belief as to whether a black cat brings good or bad luck varies in different countries. In Britain and Japan, a black cat crossing your path brings good luck, while in the United States, a black cat crossing your path is thought to bring bad luck.

Aristocats

The British National Cat Club logo was designed by Louis Wain in 1887

In the mid-19th century it became fashionable to own exotic cats, and clubs were formed to set standards and compare breeds. During the 20th century, many breeds were developed that look very different from the cat's wild ancestor. But whatever the breed, the basic behavioral patterns of cats remain the same. For a cat to be affectionate, it must be handled and talked to from birth. If kittens are reared in a cattery in large numbers and then taken from their mother at six weeks old to be placed with a family, they may appear neurotic. This is due to a lack of human contact and because they have been taken from their mother too soon.

First show
In 1871, Harrison Weir staged the first modern cat show in London. A Persian kitten won.

Fit and fluffed-up
Grooming longhaired cats is very important, particularly before a cat show. It prevents tangling and gets rid of excess hair (p. 62).

Show-off
The showing of pedigree cats, like this Birman, has probably helped to create the great variety of breeds in the world today, although many people do not agree with experimental breeding.

Red self longhair
Red self longhairs are a fairly rare breed. The beautiful red coat should show no shading or tabby markings.

Deep orange coat

Thick-set body

Ears are sometimes almost transparent

Body is muscular but elegant

The Russian blue has a wedge-shaped nose and its ears are large and slightly pointed

Russian blue

Wide-set, almost turquoise eyes

Blue beauty
The Russian blue has been called the Spanish cat and the Maltese cat, but it is widely thought to be a Russian breed. One of the most famous was Vashka, the beloved pet of Czar Nicholas I.

Long, fine-boned legs with small, oval paws

Thick, plush double coat, stands out from the cat's body because of its density

Long, tapering tail

Powerful hind legs

Large, round, copper-colored eyes

Red self longhair

Small, rounded ears

Unlucky 13
In 1898, a party of 13 dined at London's Savoy Hotel. The first guest to leave was killed soon after, fulfilling an old superstition. At the Savoy today, Kaspar, the wooden cat, always sits at the table when there are 13 diners.

The nose of the red self is so flat that the cat sometimes has trouble breathing through it

Short, solid legs

Shorthairs

Almost all cats had short hair until about 100 years ago. This was because a cat could survive and fend for itself more easily if its coat was short. Pedigree shorthaired cats fall into three main groups: the British, American, and the Oriental shorthair. The British shorthair is a stocky, muscular cat with shortish legs. The American shorthair is larger and more lithe and has slightly longer legs. Among the most popular cats today are the sleek Oriental shorthairs, which include the Siamese, Burmese, and Abyssinian breeds. There are also many nonpedigree shorthaired cats of all shapes and sizes.

American portraits, like this one by Ammi Phillips (1788–1865), often included the family pet

Sew much fun
In the early 20th century, kittens were often used to illustrate birthday cards and postcards. Kittens still enjoy playing with spools of thread today.

Abyssinian
No one knows where the graceful Abyssinian was first bred, but it looks very like the cats shown on ancient Egyptian tomb paintings. It comes in many colors including brown, sorrel (light copper), blue, fawn, lilac (pinkish-gray), and silver.

Large, pointed ears set far apart

Almond-shaped green eyes

Small, oval-shaped paws with black pads

Longish tail tipped with black

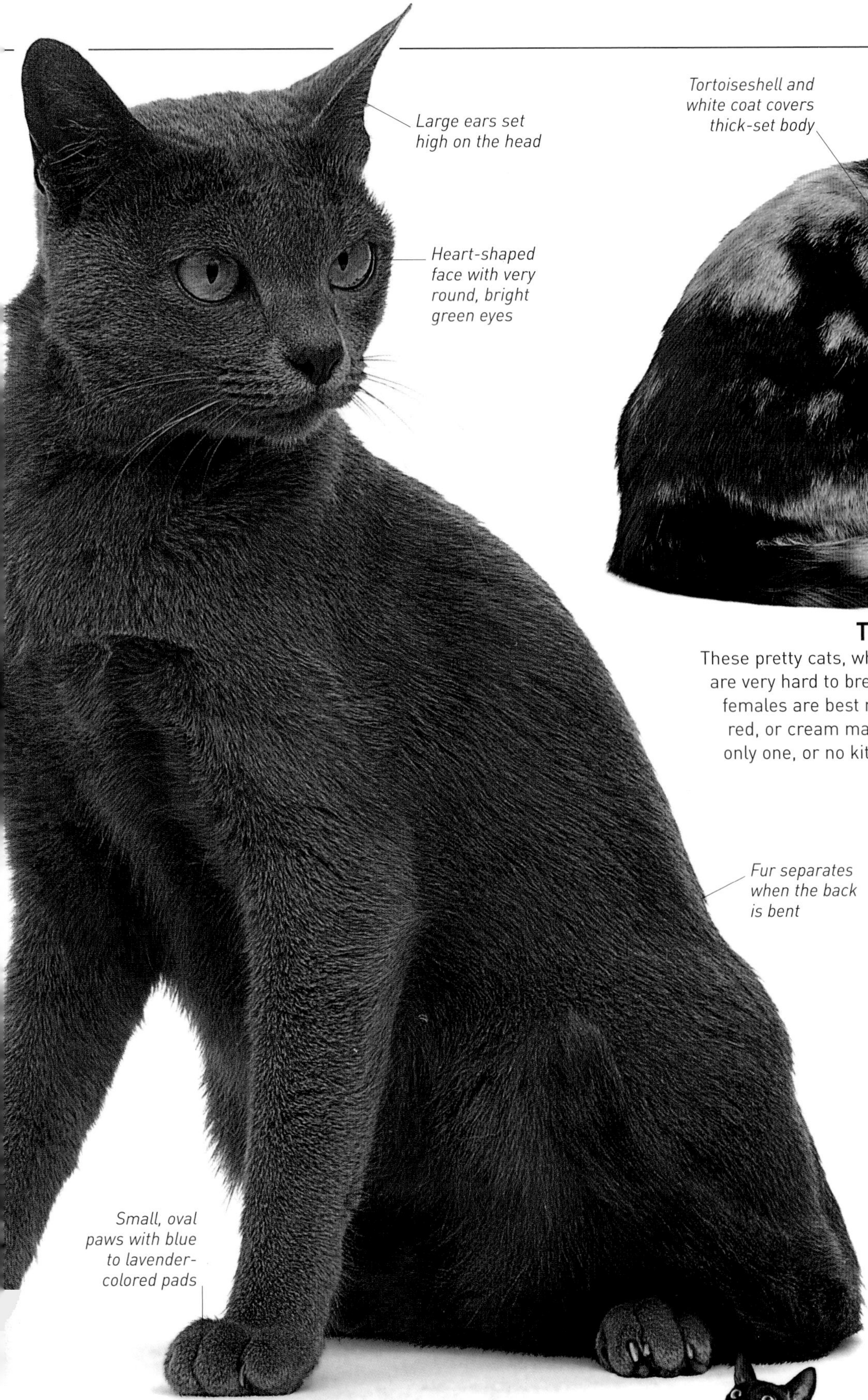

Large ears set
high on the head

Heart-shaped
face with very
round, bright
green eyes

Tortoiseshell and
white coat covers
thick-set body

Tortoiseshell and white

These pretty cats, which are almost always female,
are very hard to breed. To produce a tortoiseshell,
females are best mated to a solid-colored black,
red, or cream male, but even then there may be
only one, or no kittens with the desired coloring.

Fur separates
when the back
is bent

Small, oval
paws with blue
to lavender-
colored pads

Lookout
This tabby has found a good
perch. Nonpedigree cats
are often less nervous than
highly bred cats and usually
make good pets.

Korat
The dusky-blue korat is one
of the oldest breeds of cat and
originally comes from Thailand.
The breed was first taken to the
US in the 1950s, but did not
arrive in Britain until the 1970s.
It is a gentle, rather nervous cat.

Burmese
Like the Abyssinian, the
Burmese has a variety of coat
colors. Brown Burmese were
living in temples in Myanmar
as long ago as the 15th century.
It is an affectionate, intelligent
cat that loves to lie on beds.

Mr. and Mrs. Clark and Percy

There is no doubt that artists like painting cats. This famous painting by British artist David Hockney shows his friends Ossie Clark and Celia Birtwell with their large, white cat, Percy, taking a central role.

Dinner?

This cat can smell that there has been a bird in the cage.

Ginger-and-white cat

Ringed, fluffy tail

Mr. Mistoffelees

Old Possum's Book of Practical Cats by T. S. Eliot describes many wonderful cats. Mr. Mistoffelees (like all black cats pp. 48–49) has his own share of magic.

Miss Zoe de Bellecourt

This portrait was painted by Scottish artist George Watson (1767–1837). Cats were seen as suitable pets for young ladies.

Color change

People have tried to produce all-black and all-white versions of the Russian blue. The breed is most popular in New Zealand.

Beaten by a head

This unusual piece of American folk art, which shows a cat with a bird in its mouth, was painted perhaps as a tribute to a good hunting cat.

Siamese

Cats similar to the Siamese lived in Thailand (formerly Siam) for hundreds of years. The first Siamese came to Britain as a gift from the Court of Siam in the 1880s. They are highly intelligent, noisy cats.

Thin, tapering tail

Long, pointed ears

Tabby cat

Fluffy coat in excellent condition

Bright eyes are a sign of health

Two's company

Tabby coats are the most common markings in nonpedigree cats. Highly bred cats are often less robust than nonpedigree cats because inbreeding (p. 13) can cause physical weaknesses. These two cats clearly get along well. They are showing no aggressive signs to each other.

Long, slim legs

Small, neat paws

Longhairs

All wild cats have a two-layer fur coat (p. 14), and in cold countries, cats tend to have thicker, longer fur. But no wild cat has the luxurious fur of the longhaired domestic cat. Long hair would be a disadvantage to a wild cat because it would become matted and tangled in bushes. Among the oldest breeds of longhaired cats are the Persian and the Angora (originally from Turkey). Longhaired cats are usually placid and make excellent companions, but they do need more attention than shorthaired cats.

Birman
The Birman has a longer body than a typical longhair and similar markings to a Siamese. It may, in fact, be a cross between a Siamese and a Persian. These cats always have white feet.

Angora
This is an early engraving of an Angora, possibly the first longhair to be seen in Europe.

Large, round white paws

Neck ruff

Short head with long, pink-tipped nose

Turkish Vans
This cat is often called the Turkish swimming cat because it is fond of playing in water. It is named after the area around Lake Van in Turkey, where it has been bred for several hundred years.

Long, feathery tail

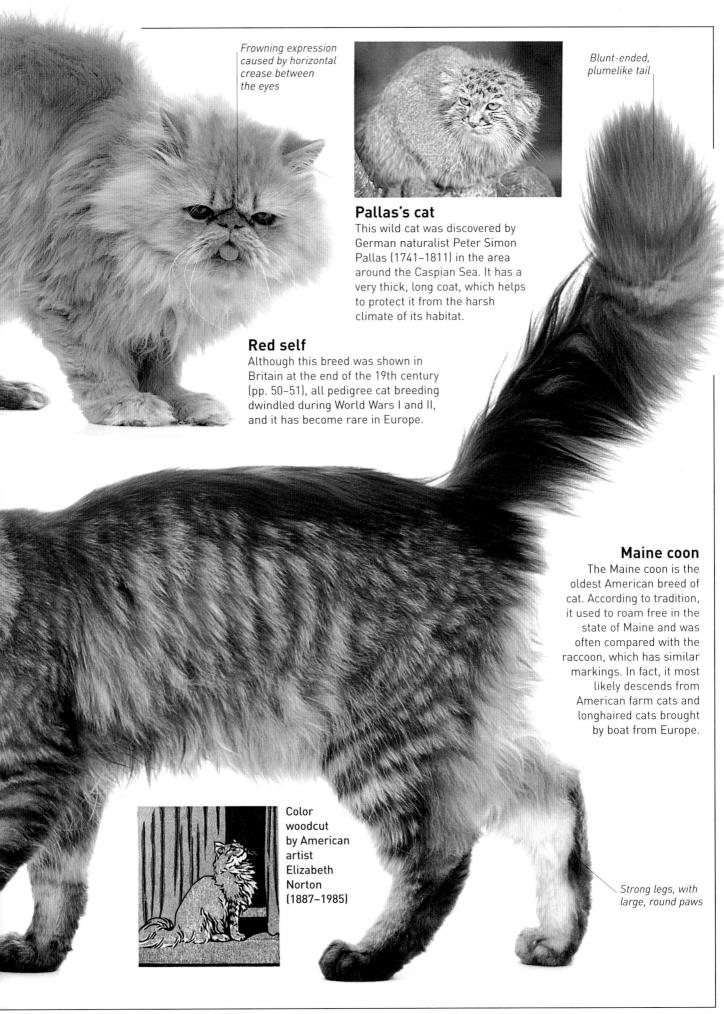

*Frowning expression
caused by horizontal
crease between
the eyes*

*Blunt-ended,
plumelike tail*

Pallas's cat

This wild cat was discovered by German naturalist Peter Simon Pallas (1741–1811) in the area around the Caspian Sea. It has a very thick, long coat, which helps to protect it from the harsh climate of its habitat.

Red self

Although this breed was shown in Britain at the end of the 19th century (pp. 50–51), all pedigree cat breeding dwindled during World Wars I and II, and it has become rare in Europe.

Maine coon

The Maine coon is the oldest American breed of cat. According to tradition, it used to roam free in the state of Maine and was often compared with the raccoon, which has similar markings. In fact, it most likely descends from American farm cats and longhaired cats brought by boat from Europe.

Color woodcut by American artist Elizabeth Norton (1887–1985)

Strong legs, with large, round paws

Cheshire cat
The British writer Lewis Carroll (1832–1898) immortalized the grinning Cheshire Cat in his book *Alice's Adventures in Wonderland*.

Curious cats

The breeding of cats for special characteristics (selective breeding) began at the start of the 20th century (pp. 50–51). Since then, many different breeds have been developed. Almost any part of the cat can be altered by selective breeding. For example, cats can be bred with very fluffy fur or a short tail. Sometimes curiosities in the wild, like the white tiger, are perfectly healthy, as are some new domestic breeds like the Burmilla, a cross between a Burmese and a chinchilla. But, all too often, excessive inbreeding produces animals with serious health issues.

The Sphynx
Hairless kittens are sometimes born due to a genetic abnormality. One such kitten, born in 1966 to a black-and-white cat, was used to develop a new breed of hairless cat called the Sphynx.

Devon rex
As a result of selective breeding, the Devon and Cornish rex cats are unique in that every hair on their bodies is soft and curly. They are healthy animals and make affectionate pets.

The curly fur is short, soft, and close-lying, with no guard hairs (p. 14)

The head is wedge-shaped with a longish nose. The ears are large and slightly rounded, and the eyes are almond-shaped

Devon rex

Even the whiskers are curly

The Owl and the Pussy Cat
A cat and bird friendship would be very unusual. But in Edward Lear's (1812–1888) poem, the owl and the pussy cat marry and live happily ever after.

Long, flexible tail

Manx
Kittens without tails can be born in any litter. Tailless cats called Manx became common on the Isle of Man off the English coast more than 200 years ago, probably as a result of the island's geographical isolation, and inbreeding (p. 13).

Defined patches of black, cream, orange, and white fur

ix 'n' match
zoos and circuses, lions and tigers ometimes mate. If the father is a lion, e cubs are called ligers and if the ger is the father, they are called gons. These animals, although ealthy, are often infertile nable to produce cubs). owever, one liger did mate uccessfully in Germany.

Manx cats can have no tail at all, a tiny bump, a moveable tail stump, or a small tail

Strong back legs

White tiger
The striking white tiger was once not uncommon in north and east central India, although there are few there now. The unusual color is a natural occurrence.

Neatly folded
Ears that turn over or hang down are rare in cats, although folded ears can occur naturally. A kitten born in Scotland with folded ears in 1961 was used to develop a new breed called the Scottish Fold.

Street life

Cat illustration by Edward Topsell, 1607

All cities have a secret world of teeming animal life. City cats find plenty of pigeons, rats, mice, and cockroaches in alleys, trash cans, and drains. City-dwelling cats have their own territories, crawling into basements, under sheds, or up onto roofs. Male city (alley) cats mark and defend their territory in the same way as pet cats and wild cats. Females also have territories, and find hidden places to have their kittens. Cats are useful in cities because they get rid of garbage and pests. The population of city cats can, however, become too large if too many people feed them. This upsets the balance of the concrete jungle.

Cats on a hot tin roof
Their roaming natures often mean that cats take to the rooftops. Here, they can escape from humans and gain access to interesting places. This delightful scene is by French artist Grandville (1803–1847).

The coat is slightly matted, a sign that this cat is not in peak condition

Tabby markings form the basic feline coat pattern

Tabby temperament
A cat's temperament is linked to the color and markings of its coat. City cats have to be calm by nature. Tabby cats and black and white cats are best suited for city life.

Street cats

[I]t is not easy to tell [th]e difference [b]etween pet cats [th]at go out at [ni]ght and street [c]ats that have [li]ttle or no [h]uman contact. [S]treet cats are [u]sually a bit [n]ervous and [s]cruffy. They [r]un away when [a]pproached and [m]ay be grubby, [w]ith torn ears and [s]ore places from [fr]equent battles.

The ear is ragged and scarred—a certain sign of battles fought

The eye is damaged, either the result of a fight or because of an inadequate diet

Tom, Dick, or Harry?

When a female cat is in heat (p. 24), several males may mate with her. This can mean that there is more than one father of the kittens in a litter, and they can all look very different, as in the painting above.

Feral cats

Feral refers to domestic animals that no longer live with humans and have returned to the wild. Some alley cats living in cities have become feral. Feral cats are often found on sparsely populated islands where they were left by sailors.

Alley cat

There is a fine line between an alley cat and a feral cat. Some alley cats can live totally outside human control, but most depend on humans in some way.

Catastrophe

This group is protesting against a proposed plan to destroy feral cats in Paris. They claim that this would upset the natural ecological balance across France.

Caring for your cat

Cats are true individuals with their own needs. If possible, every cat should be allowed outside to explore its territory and also to eat the blades of grass that help its digestion. Magnetic cat flaps allow cats maximum freedom, as the flap is opened by a magnet on the collar. Most people have their cats neutered, which prevents them from producing litters of unwanted kittens. Cats also need to be vaccinated against harmful diseases such as cat flu. Cats can live for over 20 years and need constant care, but they make very rewarding pets.

Kittens and puppies often appeared on Victorian cards

Kat kit
Regular brushing prevents cats from swallowing hair when they lick themselves. Hair forms a fur ball in the stomach, which can make the cat sick.

Water bowl

Balanced diet
Cats are carnivores and need to eat meat or fish daily. Hard cat biscuits help to keep the teeth and jaws healthy. Water is also essential.

Scratch clean
Every cat needs to stretch its body (p. 27). Mats or scratching posts are ideal for this.

Scoop

Food bowl

Gravel or commercial cat litter

Litter tray

Creature comforts
Cats are territorial and need their own sleeping place. They often choose beds or chairs because they smell reassuring.

Digging in
Nearly all cats can be trained to use a litter box. The cat buries its waste, but the litter needs to be cleaned out and changed daily,

Playtime
Cats love to play and exercise. Toys should not contain any loose string that could wind around the cat or strangle it.

Collared
Collars with an elastic strip allow the cat to escape if the collar gets caught in a branch or twig. In large towns, it is advisable to have one with an identification tag attached.

Grille can be securely fastened

On the road
Cats hate to be taken away from their own territory. Many owners leave cats in their own homes with someone coming in to feed them when they go away. If this is not possible, a secure traveling basket, with a favorite blanket in it, is important.

Basket case
Cats like to sleep in places that smell of their owner. So the cat basket should be lined with newspaper to prevent drafts and then covered with an old item of clothing as a "security blanket." Keep sleeping places free from fleas by regular spraying or washing with a special insecticide.

All you need is love
Cats need affection, and they display love for their owners in return. Cat ownership has been shown to benefit humans, particularly the old and lonely.

Did you know?

AMASING FACTS

The cat's nose pad has a unique pattern, just like a human fingerprint.

Ridged nose pad

There are more than 500 million domestic cats in the world.

A cat's heart beats nearly twice as fast as a human heart.

Cats are partially color blind, so that red colors appear green and green colors appear red.

In just seven years, a single pair of cats and their offspring could produce 420,000 kittens.

Sir Isaac Newton, who discovered the laws of gravity, also invented the cat flap.

The flat-headed cat is an expert fisher. Its webbed paws and well-developed premolars grip slippery prey well.

The domestic cat is the only cat to hold its tail vertically while walking. Wild cats hold their tails horizontally or between their legs.

A cat holding its tail tall

Cats see extremely well at dawn and dusk, which are excellent hunting times. They can see well in dim light because a layer of cells called the "tapetum lucidum" at the back of their eyes reflects light back through the retina.

A cat's ear can turn up to 180 degrees. Each ear has more than 20 muscles to control this movement.

Almost all tortoiseshell cats are female because the coloring is linked to the female sex gene.

On average, cats spend two-thirds of every day sleeping. So a nine-year-old cat has been awake for only three years of its life.

Cats "meow" often at humans, but hardly ever "meow" at other cats.

A cat nap

The spots on the back of the African cheetah are so large that they join to form striking black stripes running down its spine.

A cat cannot see things that are immediately under its nose because its nose gets in the way.

A person who killed a cat in ancient Egypt could be put to death.

The clouded leopard's canine teeth can be as long as 1¾ in (4.5 cm).

The average cat-food meal is equivalent to about five mice.

A cat hard at work grooming itself

Cats spend nearly one-third of their waking hours grooming themselves.

According to Hebrew folklore, Noah was afraid that rats would eat all the food he had stored in the ark, so God made the lion sneeze, and out popped a cat.

A cat's colorpoint pattern—where the ears, face, legs, and tail are darker than the main body—is affected by temperature. The pattern is caused by a gene that prevents color in warm parts of the body and allows color in cooler areas, such as the face, ears, and tail.

The clouded leopard

QUESTIONS AND ANSWERS

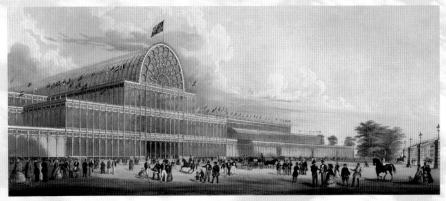
Crystal Palace, London

Q Where was the first formal cat show?

A It was held at Crystal Palace in London, UK, on July 13, 1871.

Q Why does a cat wag its tail?

A A cat will swish its tail when annoyed, move it rapidly when agitated, and twitch it when excited.

Q How well can a cat smell?

A A cat can smell another cat 330 ft (100 m) away. Cats smell with their noses, but also use the Jacobson's organ in their mouths.

Q How many claws does a cat have?

A Cats have five clawed toes on the front paws and four on the back.

Q What colors are cats' eyes?

A Cats' eyes can be copper, orange, lavender, blue, or yellow. Some cats are odd-eyed, so each eye has a different color.

Q How long do cats usually live?

A Healthy cats normally live for 12–15 years.

Cats like to rub against people

Q Why do cats rub against people's legs?

A When cats rub against people, they are marking them with their scent glands, which are between their eyes and ears, and near their tail.

Chartreux cats have orange eyes

Q How many teeth do adult cats have?

A Adult cats have a total of 30 teeth, for grasping, cutting, and shredding food. Kittens have 26 temporary teeth, which they lose when they are about six months old.

Q What makes it possible for cats to get through small spaces?

A A cat's head is its bulkiest bony structure. If it is able to get its head through, it can squeeze the rest of its body through a small gap.

Cat squeezing through a small space

Record Breakers

MOTHER TO THE MOST KITTENS
A cat named "Dusty" holds the record for the largest number of kittens. She had more than 420 kittens in her lifetime.

THE WORLD'S BEST "MOUSER"
"Towser," a tabby working on pest control in Scotland, caught 28,899 mice in 21 years—an average of about four each day.

THE LARGEST CAT BREED
The largest cat breed is the Ragdoll. Males weigh between 12 and 20 lb (5.4 and 9 kg), while females weigh between 10 and 15 lb (4.5 and 6.8 kg).

THE SMALLEST CAT BREED
The smallest cat breed is the Singapura. Males weigh about 6 lb (2.7 kg); females weigh about 4 lb (1.8 kg).

A Singapura kitten

Identifying breeds

Since selective breeding began, the look of some breeds has changed considerably. Set standards describe the ideal appearance of a breed. New breeds can result from crossing two established breeds, or a domestic cat with a small wild cat.

Pedigree or crossbreed?
A pedigree is one whose mother and father belong to the same breed. A crossbred cat has parents of different breeds.

Mother and kittens

HAIR LENGTH

Cats fall into one of three groups, depending on the length of their hair. Longhaired cats have a thick coat that can make them appear twice their actual size. The fur of shorthaired cats may be fine or coarse, and the hairs may be straight, crinkled, curly, or wavy. The Sphynx is the only pedigree breed that is "hairless."

The British blue shorthair

The "hairless" Sphynx

The Maine coon, a longhaired cat

COLORS AND PATTERNS

Over the years, selective breeding (pp. 58–59) has established a variety of different patterns and colors within the recognized breeds.

Tabby coats have symmetrical patterns of stripes and spots of a dark color on a lighter background.

Black

Tortie smoke longhair

Smoke coats have a white undercoat covered by a dark color, such as black, blue, or red.

Solid (or self) coats are one color only—black, blue, brown, cream (tan), lilac (light gray), red, or white.

Silver spotted tabby

Parti-colored coats have two or more definite colors, such as black and white. Tortoiseshell coats are black, red, and cream.

Two-toned

Shaded coats are like smoke coats except that the dark color occurs only on the tips of the hairs.

Red-shaded cameo

CAT BREEDS

The Governing Council of the Cat Fancy (GCCF) recognizes the following groups of cat breeds.

Persian longhairs
Persian longhairs have long, dense fur, flat faces, and small ears.

Orange-eyed white Persian longhair

Cream Turkish Van

Semi-longhairs
Some semi-longhairs, such as the Turkish Van, have a thinner undercoat than longhaired cats.

Cream point British shorthair

British shorthairs
British shorthairs exist in a wide range of colors and patterns. They have a large, rounded body shape and round faces.

The strongest point color is on the tail and the head

Foreign cats
This group includes a range of different cats. The Tiffanie has silky, fine hair. Asian cats have short, close-lying fur. The Ocicat has Siamese and Abyssinian ancestry. The Cornish rex has short, curly hair, and the Singapura has a ticked coat.

There are some tabby markings on the face

Burmese cats
Burmese have short, glossy fur, muscular bodies, and thin legs. They can be solid colors or tortoiseshell.

Red Tiffanie

Cream Burmese

Chocolate point Siamese

Oriental cats
Oriental shorthairs have short, glossy fur, wedge-shaped faces, big ears, and a long, tapering tail. The Angora has long, fine, silky fur, with no woolly undercoat.

The ears are big and the nose is long and straight

Pointed coats have a solid color on the main part of the cat's body, and a darker color on the extremities.

Lilac Oriental shorthair

Siamese
Siamese cats also have wedge-shaped faces and large, wide ears. They have long, light-colored bodies with darker extremities.

Ticked coats have bands of color on each hair, creating a wavy effect.

Fawn Abyssinian

Blue point Siamese

Find out more

Even if you do not have a cat of your own, there are many ways of finding out more about cats. You could join a cat club and go along to shows to learn about different breeds. You can also get information from your local animal shelter. If you find big cats interesting, visit a wildlife park to see lions, leopards, or tigers in action.

A cat of your own

If you are considering getting a cat, first investigate the kind of home and care a cat needs. The ASPCA can provide information to help you make the decision.

The judges, dressed in white, examine the cats exhibited at a show

Cat shows

Cat shows take place year round and are often open to the public. More than 1,000 cats take part in the CFA Cats! Show New York in October each year.

LONG HAIRED SECTION

Cats belonging to the club may have won many awards

Cute kittens

Pedigree kittens stay with their mothers until they are 13 weeks old, and for at least a week after they have had their vaccinations. This ensures that they are fully protected before they go to a new home.

Join a cat club

Clubs organize and take part in shows at which club members can exhibit their cats. There are hundreds of cat clubs in the United States, and the CFA can provide information and contact details for many of them.

Oriental shorthair cats have large ears and wedge-shaped heads

The kitten feels safe near its family

PLACES TO VISIT

SAN DIEGO ZOO, SAN DIEGO, CALIFORNIA
• Asian fishing cats, Pallas's cats, cheetahs, jaguars, leopards, lions, and many other cats are on display here.

BRONX ZOO, BRONX, NEW YORK
• A great zoo, with many exciting special features, including a children's zoo, Himalayan Highlands Habitat (with snow leopards), and an indoor Asian rain forest covering almost an acre.

HOUSTON ZOO, HOUSTON, TEXAS
• Home to more than 100 species of mammal, including wild cats.

PURINA FARMS, GRAY SUMMIT, MISSOURI
• Farm animals and pets are the focus of this inviting animal experience. Visitors can meet and pet different breed of cat.

THE CAT FANCIERS' ASSOCIATION CAT SHOW
• The Cat Fanciers' Association is the world's largest registry of pedigreed cats and features cat shows around the world and across the United States. Unusual breeds, from the hairless Sphynx to the rare Ocicat, may be seen at large cat shows. Check locations and dates of upcoming CFA cat shows at **www.cfa.org/shows.html**

Cats
One way to learn more about big cats is to go along to wildlife parks and talk to the keepers. Find out more from the website **www.animalsafari.com**

The animals are used to visitors in their cars

Stray cats
There are charities that take care of injured and stray cats and find suitable homes for them. Many local and state organizations, including your local ASPCA, work with volunteers to rescue thousands of cats each year.

USEFUL WEBSITES

• The ASPCA's website for children features information on caring for and enjoying your cat: **www.aspca.org/pet-care/cat-care**
• The website of the Cat Fanciers' Association explains cat breeds and cat care: **www.cfainc.org**
• National Geographic videos: **video.nationalgeographic.com/video/animals**
• Learn about tiger conservation: **www.tigersincrisis.com**
• For a wealth of information about big cats, see: **www.bornfree.org.uk**
• Discover the world's fastest cat—and conservation efforts to save the species: **www.cheetah.co.za**
• Learn about efforts to catch, spay, and release feral cats in California: **www.feralcat.com**
• Learn about the endangered mountain lion: **animals.nationalgeographic.co.in/animals/mammals/mountain-lion**
• To watch videos about big cats, go to: **www.bbc.co.uk/nature/life/Felidae**

Glossary

BREED A group of cats with particular characteristics. Humans control breeding to achieve specific features, such as coat type or head shape. If the breeding is not strictly supervised, characteristics can very quickly be lost.

CAMOUFLAGE The coloration of an animal that either blends in with the color of the surroundings or breaks up the animal's outline with stripes or spots, making it harder to see.

CANINE TEETH Four large, pointed teeth, two in the upper jaw and two in the lower. They are used to stab prey.

CARNASSIAL TEETH The teeth at the side of the jaw used for cutting off meat.

The four large canine teeth

CARNIVORE A member of the order Carnivora, which contains animals that have teeth for biting and shearing flesh. Carnivores mostly eat meat.

CATERWAUL A howling, wailing cry made by a female cat when it is in heat.

CLASS A class contains one or more orders. Cats are part of the class Mammalia.

CLAW A curved, sharp, pointed attachment to the toe. Cats draw in, or retract, their claws when they are relaxed, but can extend them quickly.

CROSSBREEDING The mating of two different breeds.

DOUBLE COAT A long topcoat over a short undercoat.

DOWN HAIR The soft, fine hair that makes up a short undercoat and provides body insulation.

FAMILY Any of the taxonomic groups into which an order is divided. A family contains one or more genera. Felidae is the name of the cat family.

FELINE Cat or catlike.

FERAL CATS Domestic cats that have returned to living in the wild and live totally outside human control.

FOLD A cat with ears that fold and turn down.

FORELEGS The front legs of a four-legged animal.

GROOM To keep neat and clan. People groom cats, but cats also spend considerable time grooming themselves with their tongues and paws.

GUARD HAIRS Long hairs that form part of the topcoat.

HABITAT The natural home of an animal or plant.

HIND LEGS The back legs of a four-legged animal.

A European wildcat

Grooming a cat at a show

INBREEDING Repeated breeding within a group of animals that are closely related to each other.

JACOBSON'S ORGAN A taste-smell organ in the roof of a cat's mouth.

KITTEN A young cat. The young of some large cats are known as cubs.

LIGAMENT The tough tissue that connects bones and cartilage.

LITTER A group of young born at one time to one female cat.

LONGHAIR A cat with a thick, long, double coat.

MANE Long hair growing on or around the neck.

NEUTER A cat that has had its reproductive organs surgically removed.

NOSE LEATHER The area of colored skin, not covered by fur, on a cat's nose.

ORDER Any of the taxonomic groups into which a class is divided. An order contains one or more families. Cats belong to the order Carnivora.

PADS The leathery areas on the feet.

PAPILLAE The hard, shiny points on a cat's tongue used for grooming.

PARTI-COLORED A cat with a coat of two or more well-defined colors.

PAW A cat's foot, with its leathery pads and sharp claws.

PEDIGREE The record of a purebred cat's ancestors.

POINTS Darker colored areas at the body's extremities— on the legs, paws, tail, head, and ears.

PURE-BREED A cat with parents belonging to the same breed. A pure-breed is also known as a pedigree cat.

PURR To make a low, vibrant sound, usually expressing pleasure. The sound is made when the bones at the base of the tongue vibrate.

SELF (or **SOLID**) A cat with a coat of only one color.

SEMI-LONGHAIR A cat with a relatively long topcoat, but a fairly thin undercoat.

SHEATHE To allow a claw to move back inside its bony, protective structure.

SHORTHAIR A cat with a short coat.

SKELETON The framework of bones that gives shape to an animal, allows the muscles to move, protects the organs, is a source of blood cells, and provides a mineral store.

A cat's tongue is covered in papillae

SMOKE A cat with a white undercoat and a darker topcoat.

SPECIES Any of the taxonomic groups into which a genus is divided. Members of the same species are able to breed with each other.

SPHYNX A breed of cat that is hairless except for a little short, downy fur usually on its extremities.

SPRAYING Using urine to mark a territory. In particular, male cats that have not been neutered do this.

STALKING To approach prey stealthily.

SUCKLE To suck milk from the mother. The term also means to give milk to a young animal.

TAXONOMY Relating to the classification of organisms into groups, based on their similarities or origin.

TENDON A band of tough tissue that attaches a muscle to a bone.

TICKED A coat in which there are bands of different color on each hair.

TOPCOAT The outer coat, made up of guard and awn hairs.

A Turkish Van pedigree cat

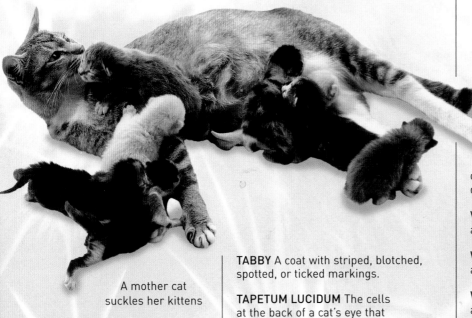

A mother cat suckles her kittens

TABBY A coat with striped, blotched, spotted, or ticked markings.

TAPETUM LUCIDUM The cells at the back of a cat's eye that reflect light.

TORTOISESHELL A cat (usually female) with black, red, and cream markings.

UNDERCOAT A coat of dense, soft fur beneath the outer, coarser fur.

VAN A coat with a white body but a colored head and tail.

WEAN When a kitten changes from a milk diet to a meat diet.

WHISKERS The stiff hairs on a cat's face, with highly sensitive nerves at their roots.

Index

Acknowledgments

Dorling Kindersley would like to thank:
Trevor Smith and all the staff at Trevor Smith's Animal World; Jim Clubb of Clubb-Chipperfield; Nicki Barrass of A1 Animals; Terry Moore of the Cat Survival Trust; the staff of the British Museum and the Natural History Museum for their assistance; Jacquie Gulliver and Lynne Williams for their work on the initial stages of the book; Christian Sévigny and Liz Sephton for design assistance; Claire Gillard and Céline Carez for editorial assistance.

For this relaunch edition the publishers would also like to thank: Hazel Beynon for text editing and Carron Brown for proofreading.

The publisher would like to thank the following for their kind permission to reproduce their photographs:
a=above t=top b=bottom l=left r=right c=center

Animals Unlimited: 53b; Ardea: R.Beames 40c; K. Fink 40tr; Bridgeman Art Library: back jacket bl above, 28tc, 62tl; Bibliothèque Nationale, Paris 28tb; Chadwick Gallery, Warwicks 52c; National Gallery, London 30tl detail; National Gallery of Scotland 54bl; Victoria & Albert Museum, London 20tl; Courtesy of the Trustees of the British Museum: 6tr, 22bl, 31tr; In the Collection of the Duke of Buccleuch & Queensberry KT: 16cr detail; Jean Loup Charmet: 7tr; Bruce Coleman Ltd: 57cr; Jen & Des Bartlett 13c, 23bl, 25c, 28c; Jane Burton 16cb; Jane Burton & Kim Taylor 16cl; Eric Creighton 26cl; Gerald Cubitt 39br, 43b; G. D. Plage 24cl; Hans Reinhard 12c, 16tl, 24bl, 37tc, 42–43; Norman Tomalin 45bl; Konrad Wothe 22br; Rod Williams 11c, 33cb; Gunter Ziesler 42c, 43tl; E.T. Archive: 24tr, 62br, © Sheila Roberts 1971, 63tc; Mary Evans Picture Library: 10cl, 19t, 27cr, 49tl, tr, 58br; Werner Forman Archive: 33b, 35tr; Freer Gallery of Art, Washington: 21tl detail, Acc. No. 04.357; Robert Harding Picture Library: 49bl; Marc Henrie: 50cl; "Mr. & Mrs. Clark & Percy" 1970-1, © David Hockney/photo Tate Gallery: 54tl; Michael Holford: front jacket tr & tl below, 31tl, c, 35b, 37c, 47tr, 47br, 48cl; Hulton-Deutsch Collection: 30b; Hutchison Library: 34c; Image Bank: 54cl; Images Colour Library: 47bl, 48tl, 58tl; Kobal Collection: 11cl, 22t, 49cr; M.R. Long: 9c; LYNX: 36tr; Mansell Collection: 13bl; Metropolitan Museum of Art: 57b; Museum of American Folk Art: 52t; National Gallery of Art, Washington: 55tr (gift of Edgar William & Bernice Chrysler Garbisch); Natural History Museum: 8tl, bl, 12bl, 13tl, br, 33c, 35c, 36cr, 37c, 38c; Natural History Photographic Agency: Agence Nature 18bl; Anthony Bannister 42b; Nigel Dennis 45tl; Patrick Fagot 19c; Peter Johnson 14cl, 45cl; Stephen Krasman 16tr; Gérard Lacz 12tl, 58tr, 59bl; Northampton Historical Society, Mass.: 15tc; Oxford Scientific Films: 37tl, 39tl; Roy Coombes 27c; Sean Morris 41b; Richard Packwood 12cb; Kjell Sandved 59br; Bernard Schellhammer 53cr; Quadrant Picture Library: 42cb; Courtesy of The Savoy: 51cr; Scala: Palazzo Medici Riccardi, Florence 32bl detail; Museo Nazionale, Napoli 46tl; National Museum, Athens 47tl; Spectrum Colour Library: 8br; Frank Spooner Pictures: 61br; Survival Anglia; Dieter & Mary Plage 32tl; Alan Root 27tr; Maurice Tibbles 14tr; Amoret Tanner: 28tl; Victoria & Albert Museum Picture Library: 43tr detail; Zefa: 16ct; E. & P. Bauer 23bl, 38bl; M. N. Boulton 11bl; Bramaz 63br; G. Dimijian 21cr; D. Kessel 35tl; Lummerc 20br; Orion 19cb Ardea London 1tc: John Daniels 64tl, 68crb; Masahiro Iijima 64br; Corbis: Tom Brakefield 66–67; Roy Morsch 68–69; John Periam /Cordaiy Photo Library Ltd 69bc; DK Images: Gables 70–71; Jerry Young 70bc; Longleat Safari Park, Wiltshire: 69clb; Masterfile UK: 68cl; Oxford Scientific Films: Richard Packwood 71tc; Rex Features: John Gooch 68–69tc. Philip Berry;Frank lane picture agency 65-65 All other images © Dorling Kindersley Illustrations by: Dan Wright

All other images © Dorling Kindersley.
For further information see:
www.dkimages.com